ANGELS IN CLASSICAL ART

Angels in Classical Art

---

50 Frameable 8" x 10" Prints of Beautiful, Angelic Artwork

THE LIVING ROOM ART GALLERY SERIES

Compiled & Introduced by Greg Fox

OTHER BOOKS by GREG FOX

The Classical Male Figure: 50 Frameable 8" x 10" Prints of Exquisite, Historical Male Figure Art

Kyle's Bed & Breakfast

Kyle's Bed & Breakfast: A Second Bowl of Serial

Kyle's Bed & Breakfast: Hot off the Griddle

Kyle's Bed & Breakfast: Without Reservations

Kyle's B&B Presents: Drawings of Drew

The Sugar Maple Press Anthology of Nature Poems (editor)

Dedicated, with love,
to Eleanor and Sheila

FRONT COVER: "Angel" - Abbott Handerson Thayer - 1887
BACK COVER: "Archangel Michael Hurls the Rebellious Angels into the Abyss" - Luca Giordano - 1666
OPPOSITE TITLE PAGE: "Love on the Lookout" - Louis-Jean-Francois Lagrenee - 1779

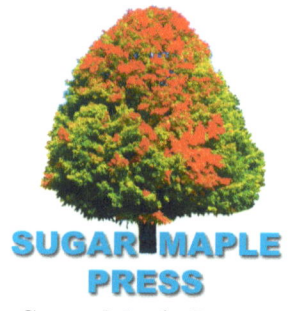

Sugar Maple Press

www.sugarmaplepress.com

e-mail: sugarmaplepress@yahoo.com

Sugar Maple Press edition: Copyright © 2016 by Greg Fox

All rights reserved. No part of this book may be reproduced in any form or by any means without prior written consent of the Publisher, excepting brief quotes used in reviews.

All Sugar Maple Press titles are available at special quantity discounts for bulk purchases, for sales promotions, premiums, fundraising, educational or institutional use.
Contact us at sugarmaplepress@yahoo.com for details.

ISBN-13: 978-0692685044
ISBN-10: 0692685049

First Sugar Maple Press Trade Paperback Printing: Spring, 2016

Introduction

When I launched the **Living Room Art Gallery** series of books earlier this year, one of the volumes I was most looking forward to doing was one featuring the art of angels. From as early as I can remember, I've always had a "thing" for angels, and as I was growing up I became accustomed to the traditional imagery of angels...wings, halos, white flowing robes. This is the imagery of angels we've come to know in western art for centuries now, but that wasn't always the case.

Angels, in one form or another, have appeared in various religious traditions for thousands of years. While the way in which they have been portrayed in art has varied, it wasn't until the late 4th century AD that the wings began to appear on angels in Christian art, not coincidentally around the same time that the Roman empire was shifting from paganism to Christianity. There appears to be some overlap in angelic imagery with the winged Roman goddess Victoria, (Victory), herself an adaptation of the winged Greek goddess Nike. And then Byzantine art, in particular, developed the idea of the archangel Michael being depicted in military garb/battle gear.

During the Middle Ages, angels took on a somewhat formalized look... the archangels being depicted in brightly colored vestments, and the lower-ranked angels usually appearing in white robes. Gender has always been a bit fluid with angels; some schools of thought indicated that angels were genderless, and should be depicted as such. Even in the most feminine looking angels, they are not usually depicted by artists as having breasts, but instead appear to be androgynous beings. However, other artists have ignored that credo, and have portrayed angels as very clearly either male or female.

As the Italian Renaissance dawned, the appearance of the putto, (plural putti), became more frequent in angelic art. Often confused with "cherubs" or "cherubim", (which ac-

"Eos" - Evelyn De Morgan - 1895

tually happen to be somewhat intimidating looking four-faced angels), the putti are the Cupid-like winged infant angels, (such as those depicted in the Raphael painting at left). And, as you'll see in this book, they've played a big, often playful part in much angelic artwork from the 1400s onward.

The focus of this book is mainly western angelic art in what I refer to as the "Classical period".... roughly from the late Middle Ages up until about 1920. You will see a wide range of styles... from the very formal, (but still beautiful!), representations by Guariento di Arpo of the archangel Michael from the mid 1300s, (the oldest piece in the book), and the Annunciation by Fra Angelico in

"Two Putti(detail from the Sistine Madonna)" - Raphael - 1512-1513

Continued >>

the 1420s...through the warmer, more evocative imagery in the 1500s by Titian and Caravaggio...up through the stunning, almost romantic quality of William-Adolphe Bouguereau and Abbot Handerson Thayer in the late 1800s. Even Van Gogh is represented here, in a piece from 1889, a beautiful post-Impressionist work from the year before he died.

My own background in art, at least professionally, is through my comics illustration work. Although I'm known primarily for a syndicated comic strip I currently write & draw called *Kyle's Bed & Breakfast*, I also wrote and drew a comic strip about an

A typical scene from **An Angel's Story**...*Steve stopping to offer some angelic roadside assistance.*

angel named Steve, (yes, really), for about nine years called *An Angel's Story*. With this angel, there was not much of an ambivalence about his gender; he was very clearly a guy. And also not the most traditional, in terms of demeanor. For the first few years of the strip, at least, be was very much an angel-in-training. But readers fell in love with Steve the angel during that nine year run, (1994-2003), so much so that I bring him back for appearances every year around Christmas in *Kyle's Bed & Breakfast*. (I've included some excerpts here on this page, both from *An Angel's Story* and also from one of Steve's appearances in *Kyle's Bed & Breakfast*). This is just another reason why I feel a connection to angels, and I know first-hand, from the wealth of cards, letters, and e-mails I received, (and still receive!), about Steve the angel, how much people around the world care about angels, too. I believe there is something in angels that inspires us all to be our best selves...our most caring and kind selves. And I think having beautiful images of angels, as you'll find in this book, to decorate your home and workspace with, can only help to bring more light and beauty and sweetness into the world.

That is why I am delighted to be able to present this book, which gives folks a very affordable way to adorn their home or workspace with lots of sumptuous angelic artwork. As stated in the title, this is a book of hang-able, frame-able prints, but you don't need to hang them. The book functions equally well as a coffee-table book, to enjoy the artwork in book form for years to come. If you do choose to hang & frame these, though, you'll be happy to know all of the works here are sized to fit into 8" x 10" frames, probably the most common, (and inexpensive), pre-made frame size. So you won't need to spend exorbitant amounts of money having any custom frames made for these. (Tips on how to remove prints from this book, and also tips on where to buy low-cost, quality frames, are on page 107 at the back of this book).

I hope this book brings beauty & joy into your life, and if you like it, that you'll check out some of the other volumes in the **Living Room Art Gallery** series from Sugar Maple Press. But for now, let's get started with this grand volume of classic angelic artwork.

Greg Fox
April, 2016

The angel Steve shows up on Christmas Eve in **Kyle's Bed & Breakfast** *to offer some more angelic insights. (Greg Fox © 2016)*

OPPOSITE PAGE:
TITLE: Archangel Gabriel   ARTIST: Titian
YEAR: 1522

A NOTE ABOUT ORIENTATION: The first 41 prints in this book are meant to be viewed/framed/hung vertically, ("portrait style")...and the final 9 prints are meant to be viewed/framed/hung horizontally, ("landscape style"). So, to view those last 9 prints in this book, simply rotate the book 90 degrees clockwise.

OPPOSITE PAGE:
TITLE: Winged Figure
ARTIST: Abbot Handerson Thayer
YEAR: 1889

OPPOSITE PAGE:
TITLE: The Archangel Michael
ARTIST: Pietro Perugino
YEAR: circa 1500

OPPOSITE PAGE:
TITLE: Playing Putto-Musician Angel
ARTIST: Rosso Fiorentino
YEAR: 1518

OPPOSITE PAGE:
TITLE: Annunciation
ARTIST: Fra Angelico
YEAR: circa 1426

OPPOSITE PAGE:
TITLE: An Angel Playing a Flageolet
ARTIST: Edward Burne-Jones
YEAR: 1878

OPPOSITE PAGE:
TITLE: Elijah in the Wilderness
ARTIST: Frederic Leighton
YEAR: 1878

OPPOSITE PAGE:
TITLE: Leveil du coeur-The Hearts Awakening
ARTIST: William-Adolphe Bouguereau
YEAR: 1892

OPPOSITE PAGE:
TITLE: An Angel Appears to the Israelites
ARTIST: Gustav Dore
YEAR:1866

OPPOSITE PAGE:
Unknown Artist-French
YEAR: 1600s-1700s

OPPOSITE PAGE:
TITLE: Allegory of Wealth
ARTIST: Simon Vouet
YEAR: 1630-1635

OPPOSITE PAGE:
TITLE: Musician Angel from fresco paintings of the Basilica dei Santi Apostoli
ARTIST:Melozzo da Forli
YEAR: 1480

OPPOSITE PAGE:
TITLE: The Annunciation-the Angel
ARTIST: Jacopo Tintoretto
YEAR: between 1560 - 1585

OPPOSITE PAGE:
TITLE: Angels Descending
ARTIST: Rupert Bunny
YEAR: circa 1897

OPPOSITE PAGE:
TITLE: A Soul Taken Away by an Angel
ARTIST: Jean-Leon Gerome
YEAR: 1853

OPPOSITE PAGE:
TITLE: The Dream of St Joseph
ARTIST: Anton Raphael Mengs
YEAR: 1773-1774

OPPOSITE PAGE:
TITLE: The Archangel Uriel-Mosaic
ARTIST: James Powell and Sons of the Whitefriars Foundry
YEAR: 1888

OPPOSITE PAGE:
TITLE: Immortality
ARTIST: Henri Fantin-Latour
YEAR: 1889

OPPOSITE PAGE:
TITLE: The Shepherds and the Angel
ARTIST: Carl Heinrich Bloch
YEAR: 1879

OPPOSITE PAGE:
TITLE: Blessed Soul
ARTIST: Guido Reni
YEAR: 1640

OPPOSITE PAGE:
TITLE: Archangel Michael Hurls the Rebellious Angels into the Abyss
ARTIST: Luca Giordano
YEAR: 1666

OPPOSITE PAGE:
TITLE: The Adoration of the Christ Child
ARTIST: Follower of Jan Joest of Kalkar
YEAR: 1515

OPPOSITE PAGE:
TITLE: Angel Bust
ARTIST: Raphael
YEAR: between 1500-1501

OPPOSITE PAGE:
TITLE: De Tijd-The Time
ARTIST: Pieter Christoffel Wonder
YEAR: 1810

OPPOSITE PAGE:
TITLE: The Queen of the Angels
ARTIST: William-Adolphe Bouguereau
YEAR: 1900

OPPOSITE PAGE:
TITLE: Winged Figure
ARTIST: Frederick Bosley
YEAR: 1913

OPPOSITE PAGE:
TITLE: The Voyage of Life- Old Age
ARTIST: Thomas Cole
YEAR: 1840

OPPOSITE PAGE:
TITLE: The Guardian Angel
ARTIST: Marcantonio Franceschini
YEAR: 1716

OPPOSITE PAGE:
TITLE: Archangel Michael
ARTIST: Guariento di Arpo
YEAR: 1300s

OPPOSITE PAGE:
TITLE: Song of the Angels
ARTIST: William-Adolphe Bouguereau
YEAR: 1881

OPPOSITE PAGE:
TITLE: Half Figure of an Angel, after Rembrandt
ARTIST: Vincent van Gogh
YEAR: 1889

OPPOSITE PAGE:
TITLE: Christ in Gethsemane
ARTIST: Carl Heinrich Bloch
YEAR: 1873

OPPOSITE PAGE:
TITLE: The Vision of the Four Chariots
ARTIST: Gustav Dore
YEAR: 1866

OPPOSITE PAGE:
TITLE: The Annunciation
ARTIST: Gerard David
YEAR: 1506

OPPOSITE PAGE:
TITLE: Genius of Art
ARTIST: Karl Bryullov
YEAR: 1817

OPPOSITE PAGE:
TITLE: L'Assaut (The Assault)
ARTIST: William-Adolphe Bouguereau
YEAR: 1898

OPPOSITE PAGE:
TITLE: Musician Angel from fresco paintings of the Basilica dei Santi Apostoli
ARTIST: Melozzo da Forli
YEAR: 1480

OPPOSITE PAGE:
TITLE: Tobías y el ángel
ARTIST: Francisco Goya
YEAR: 1787

OPPOSITE PAGE:
TITLE: Winged Figure Seated upon a Rock
ARTIST: Abbott Handerson Thayer
YEAR: between 1903-1916

OPPOSITE PAGE:
TITLE: The Resurrection
ARTIST: Carl Heinrich Bloch
YEAR: 1873

OPPOSITE PAGE:
TITLE: Angel
ARTIST: Abbott Handerson Thayer
YEAR: 1887

OPPOSITE PAGE:
TITLE: Drei Engel
ARTIST: Franz Kadlik
YEAR: 1822

OPPOSITE PAGE:
TITLE: Saint Francis of Assisi in Ecstasy
ARTIST: Caravaggio
YEAR: circa 1595

OPPOSITE PAGE:
TITLE: Saint Cecilia Accompanied by Angels
ARTIST: Simon Glücklich
YEAR: 1886

OPPOSITE PAGE:
TITLE: The Liberation of Saint Peter
ARTIST: Antonio de Bellis
YEAR: early 1640s

OPPOSITE PAGE:
TITLE: Detail from Tobias and the Angel
ARTIST: Giovanni Girolamo Savoldo
YEAR: 1530

OPPOSITE PAGE:
TITLE: Fallen Angel
ARTIST: Alexandre Cabanel
YEAR: 1868

OPPOSITE PAGE:
TITLE: Aurora Triumphans
ARTIST: Evelyn de Morgan
YEAR: 1877-1878

OPPOSITE PAGE:
TITLE: Equality Before Death
ARTIST: William Bouguereau
YEAR: 1848

OPPOSITE PAGE:
TITLE: Saint Catherine Carried by the Angels
ARTIST: Karl von Blaas
YEAR: between 1860

Coming soon from
Sugar Maple Press

An Angel's Story
The Collection

Featuring all of the comic strip adventures of Steve the angel. (May be available by the time you are reading this!)

Keep up with
An Angel's Story
on Facebook at
www.facebook.com/anangelsstory

And see other titles available from
Sugar Maple Press
2 pages ahead!

PAGE REMOVAL SUGGESTIONS:

So, you want to frame some of these beautiful art prints and get 'em up on your walls to beautify your home or workplace? Cool! Here are 2 methods to get individual pages out of this book smoothly & easily. I prefer method # 1, but if that seems too tricky, (or if you're at all nervous about or unskilled with using a razor blade), try method # 2.

Method # 1

What you'll need:

- A sharp cutting tool, such as an X-acto knife, box cutter, or even a fresh razor blade.
- A thin, solid surface to place behind the page you're going to remove from the book. It must be longer than the height of the book, (11 inches). A thin metal ruler would be ideal. If you don't have that, a thin manila folder or very thin piece of cardboard will do, as long as it's slightly longer than 11 inches).
- If you're at all nervous about cutting yourself with that razor, a pair of semi-heavy work gloves, (check out Home Depot for a large variety).

Now follow these directions:

1. Place the book on a firm table surface in front of you, and open it to the page of the art print you want to remove from the book.
2. Now, turn the page one page ahead, and place your thin solid surface, (the metal ruler or manila folder), on that page.
3. Push the metal ruler/manila folder as far into the inner center binding of the book as you can, and hold it there in place.
4. Turn back to the page of the art print you want to remove, so that the art print is now facing you, and the metal ruler/manila folder is directly behind it, pressed into the inner center binding of the book.
5. Now, with the book held open as WIDE as you can manage, **VERY CAREFULLY**, take your sharp cutting tool, and, (placing it as close as you can to the inner center binding of the book), beginning at the bottom of the page, slice upward to the top of the page. Be sure to make the slice as CLOSE to the inner center binding of the book as you can
6. Once you've removed the page from the book…take a deep breath. You did it!

Method # 2

What you'll need:

- String, (just some plain white string, like kite string or any string, really, as long as it's clean).
- A glass of clean water.

Now follow these directions:
1. Cut a length of string longer than the book's height, (11 inches.... cut it to about 14 inches, so there's extra to hold on to).
2. Soak the string in the glass of clean water. It needs to be wet, although it shouldn't be dripping wet, as that may be too much. Just get it nice and wet, but not dripping.
3. Open the book to the page of the art print you want to remove. Place the wet string **along the very inner center binding** of the book on that page; pull it tight so it is straight, very firmly tucked into the inner binding, **as close to the inner spine as possible**, (this is **important**!).
4. Close the book and hold it tightly closed for about 15 seconds.
5. Now open the book, remove the string and examine the page. There should be a line where the string was where it is wet, and therefore very weak.
6. Now carefully tear the page out . It should tear cleanly on the line. if not, wet the string more and put it back on the already weak area and do it again. (The edge of the page you tore may look a little ragged, but that's OK... that part will be hidden under the matte part of the frame).

Why do I NOT prefer this method? Well, I'm a bit nervous about getting any kind of water near my books, and while this amount of water is miniscule and should not damage the rest of the book, it still makes me a little nervous about long term effects on the book itself. However, if you're planning to frame ALL or most of the art prints in the book, and saving the book itself is not important, then by all means, I would use this method. (You can always buy another copy of this book if you want to have it in book form, while also having the prints hanging on your wall!).

A quick note about FRAMING and HANGING these art-prints ...…

The frame size you'll need to frame these is the standard 8" x 10" picture-frame; the kind that have a matte inside, which actually allows for a slightly smaller viewing area of 7 and 3/8" x 9 and 3/8". This is a very standard frame size, probably the most common size you'll find in stores, (and conveniently, the right size for ALL of the art-prints in this book!). My advice… if you happen to have a **Michael's** arts & crafts store in your area, they have a wonderful selection of frames, at very affordable prices, (which often go on sale… it may pay to check their sale flyer for several weeks before buying. I've often bought frames there at 50% off!).

After you've (very carefully) removed the art print you want to frame from this book, just center it within the cardboard matte that comes with your frame, (hint: use a couple of pieces of low-resistant artist's or painter's tape to hold it in place), place it within your frame, and you're all set!

When choosing a wall on which to hang your art print, (and this goes for **all** other prints, photos, and original artwork, too, that you may want to hang in your home or workspace), always choose a surface that does **not** get hit by **direct sunlight,** as that could eventually fade the print/photo/artwork. You may need to take a few days to check a wall surface at various times of the day, as some areas may only get exposed to direct sunlight for a few hours a day, such as early morning or late afternoon, which can still be damaging. (This is especially important for o**riginal artwork**... because if an art print or photo gets sun-damaged, you could always buy another book of prints or photos to replace it... but once original artwork is damaged, it's irreplaveable). Now you know all you need to know to beautify your home or workspace with inspiring artwork!!!

ALSO AVAILABLE from SUGAR MAPLE PRESS

KYLE'S BED & BREAKFAST

The long-running syndicated comic strip **Kyle's Bed & Breakfast**, the addictively fun-filled series focused on the lives of a group of quirky, (and often hunky!), gay men living in a harbor town B&B in the northeastern USA, is collected here for the first time in this volume. See how it all started, as Kyle opens up his new B&B in Northport, and before long, it's brimming with new guests, lots of drama, laughter, romance, intrigue, and the occasional tear! Watch as all of the guys meet each other for the first time. Included also is a never-before-published 2 page episode, and also a 9-page blueprints section showing exactly how the house is laid out! When this collection was first released, it became a **Lambda Literary Award Finalist** for "Best Humor Book of the Year"! Available now at your local bookstore, and at Amazon.com

150 PAGES • BLACK & WHITE

KYLE'S BED & BREAKFAST
A Second Bowl of Serial

The B&B boys are back for more romance, drama, laughter, and pure wackiness in their second collection of adventures! Starting up right where the first book left off, join the guys as some new faces arrive at the B&B, (like Breyer, Matt and Dave), and new romances catch fire, (some fleeting, and some more substantial!). Included also is a never-before-seen anywhere else 3-episode adventure that is sure to touch your heart! Available now at your local bookstore, and at Amazon.com

142 PAGES • BLACK & WHITE

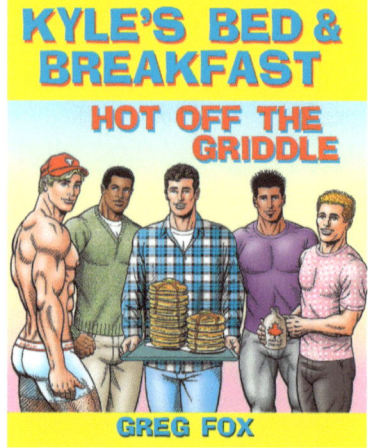

KYLE'S BED & BREAKFAST
Hot Off the Griddle

The B&B stories continue, more vibrantly than ever as this volume marks the beginning of the strip's run in FULL COLOR! Starting up right where the second book left off, join the guys as even more new faces arrive at the B&B, (like Njord, Morgan, Kristian and the infamous Price!), and the long awaited return of Jeff Olsen! Included also is a never-before-seen anywhere else new episode, and to top it off, see the debut of the B&B's own beloved Siberian Husky, Frosty! Available now at your local bookstore, and at Amazon.com

120 PAGES • FULL COLOR

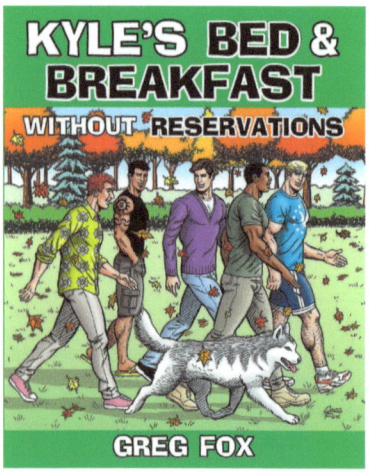

KYLE'S BED & BREAKFAST
Without Reservations

And the B&B stories continue! Once again in full color, we meet some more new arrivals, including Rudy, Olympic figure skater Michael, and the debut of the super-popular Alabama muscle-bear himself...Drew Danvers! Not to mention, a certain couple get engaged! Also included in this volume is an all-new, never before published seven page story that is sure to touch your heart! Available through your local bookstore, and at Amazon.com

102 PAGES • FULL COLOR

ALSO AVAILABLE from SUGAR MAPLE PRESS

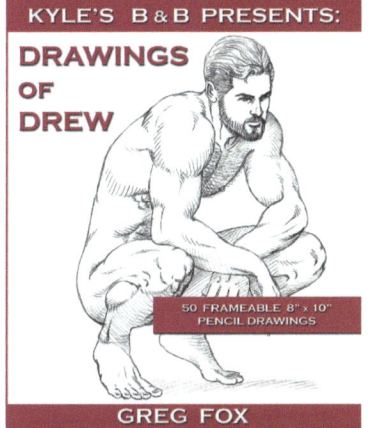

KYLE'S B & B PRESENTS:
Drawings of Drew

This collection of classical style figure drawings of Drew is directly inspired by a storyline within the Kyle's B&B comic strip; these are the pictures of Drew from when he posed for figure drawings while he was in graduate school in Alabama. 50 beautiful pencil drawings of Drew, make for a collection that every fan of Kyle's B&B must own! Available through your local bookstore, and at Amazon.com

132 PAGES • BLACK & WHITE

MORE TITLES in THE LIVING ROOM ART GALLERY SERIES
ALSO AVAILABLE from SUGAR MAPLE PRESS

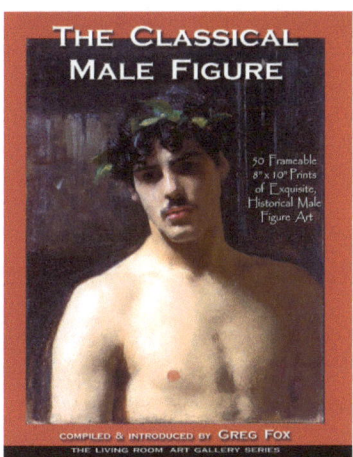

THE CLASSICAL MALE FIGURE
50 Frameable 8" x 10" Prints of Exquisite, Historical Male Figure Art

The first volume in the **Living Room Art Gallery** series features masterpieces of art focused on the male figure through the ages, including artists such as John Singer Sargent, Thomas Eakins, Michelangelo, Jean-Auguste-Dominique Ingres, Jacques Louis David, William Etty, Harold Knight, William-Adolphe Bouguereau and many more.

110 PAGES • FULL COLOR

UPCOMING TITLES, (which may be available by the time you read this), INCLUDE: **CLASSIC MEN** (Clothed Male Figure) • **THE CLASSICAL FEMALE FIGURE** • **CLASSIC WOMEN** (Clothed Female Figure) and many more to come! Check Amazon.com for new releases, and keep up with us on **Facebook** at the **Classical Male Figure Facebook Page** at www.facebook.com/classicalmalefigure

ACKNOWLEDGEMENTS

There are so many to thank for helping this book come to be. Starting with

- My mother, Eleanor, whose life was filled with appreciation of art and made our home an art-filled, beautiful, warm place to live. I miss you every day!
- Aunt Sheila, who was such an empowering, artful influence on me all throughout my life… I miss you every day, too!
- The rest of my family, in New York, California, and beyond. Thank you for your love and belief in me.
- Book Revue bookstore in Huntington, Long Island, NY. My "second home" for so many years!
- My friends far and wide… from Huntington, Geneseo, Spize, Sam Ash, Northport, Book Revue, the Berndt Toast gang, Prism Comics, the Comic Con circuit and elsewhere. Thank you for lifting me up and making me smile!
- For the many artists whose amazing work is featured in this book. Thank you for sharing your tremendous talent, which brought light into this world… I am deeply honored to be able to present your work once again for the world to appreciate!
- Kathy O'Marra, for being such a strong supporter of my work all these years. And for being a great friend!
- My friend Grant Thatcher, for not flinching when I continually asked for his opinion on yet another cover design!!!
- Misty, Ginger, and Midnight
- Marianne Williamson, for your inspiration and for being a sparkling light in this world.
- The readers of Kyle's B&B. Thank you for your love and support of my art… I am deeply, deeply grateful.
- Jesus, the Holy Spirit, and all of the Angels and saints!
- God, for all of the love, light, and joy. And for so many miracles along the way!

♥ KEEP YOUR LOVE ALIVE ♥

If you happen to be looking for any organizations that are doing good work in the world, here are just a few, (of many), that I heartily encourage you to visit their websites and find out more about:

- www.doctorswithoutborders.org   **Doctors Without Borders,** (Médecins Sans Frontières), Providing emergency medical care around the world in desperate situations.

- www.oxfamamerica.org   **Oxfam** is an international confederation of 15 organizations working in more than 90 countries worldwide to find lasting solutions to poverty and related injustice around Providing emergency medical care around the world in desperate situations.

- www.glwd.org   **God's Love We Deliver** is the tri-state area's, (NY, NJ, CT). leading provider of nutritious, individually-tailored meals to people who are too sick to shop or cook for themselves.

- www.outrightinternational.org   **OutRight Action International** (formerly the International Gay & Lesbian Human Rights Campaign)

- www.TheHungerSite.com   (Click & Donate Free Food!)

- www.gmhc.org   **The Gay Men's Health Crisis** (GMHC) is a NYC-based non-profit, volunteer-supported and community-based AIDS service organization that has led the United States in the fight against AIDS.

- www.whyhunger.org   **Why Hunger** (formerly World Hunger Year). Working to eradicate world hunger.

- www.nrdc.org   (**National Resource Defense Council**) NRDC's mission is to safeguard the Earth: its people, its plants and animals and the natural systems on which all life depends.

ABOUT GREG FOX

Greg Fox began making comics at 12 years old, publishing his first strip at age 14 in his high school newspaper and continuing to illustrate and write comic strips through high school and college. He received a B.A. from Geneseo College in upstate New York. Immediately following college, he played guitar in several New York-based rock bands, but then jumped into doing comics full-force. His illustration work has appeared in comic books for a number of companies, including Triumphant Comics, and Marvel Comics, and in magazines such as Blue, the Advocate, Genre, D.J. Times, Music & Sound Retailer, and many others. He is also the writer/artist for such comic strips as "**Manic Music**", (based on his experience in the rock music world), and "**An Angel's Story**".

Fox's most notable comic strip, "**Kyle's Bed & Breakfast**", premiered in late 1998. The strip is currently syndicated to a variety of publications across North America, and also has a worldwide following on the web. Since 2004, Fox has published 4 book collections of Kyle's B&B, (one of which was a Lambda Literary Award Finalist), and an addictional volume of classical-style figure drawings of Drew Danvers, one of the characters in Kyle's B&B, He was the grand-prize winner of the "Life Without Fair Courts" cartoon contest in 2007, sponsored by Lambda Legal. **The Sugar Maple Press Anthology of Nature Poems**, published in Spring of 2014, featured Greg Fox as editor and photographer. The fourth collection of Kyle's B&B ,"Kyle's Bed & Breakfast: Without Reservations" was published in November, 2015.

Fox currently resides in Northport, Long Island, New York, busily working on new episodes of Kyle's B&B, and several other book projects for **Sugar Maple Press**, including new volumes of the **Living Room Art Gallery Series**, as well as the fifth volume of the Kyle's Bed & Breakfast series.

He can be reached at: gregfox727@gmail.com

His work can be seen at www.kylecomics.com

Thank You!

www.ingramcontent.com/pod-product-compliance
Lightning Source LLC
Chambersburg PA
CBHW042011150426
43195CB00003B/94